Where Are We Going?

Written by Ellen Mayes-Stemple

Peter's dad said, "For your birthday we can go on a trip wherever you want."

"AND," Peter's dad said, "you can bring your best friend Joe."

So Peter and Joe talked about where they might go.

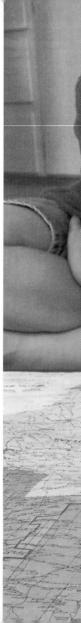

Peter said, "I think we should go to the White House and visit the President."

"I think we should take a
balloon ride and pretend we are
great explorers. The President
could come with us," chatted Joe.

5

Peter said, "I know! We could go to the Alamo and learn about Texas history."

"I know! We should go to a dude ranch and ride horses, herd cattle, and be real cowboys," babbled Joe.

Peter said, "I think we should go down South and look at all the old mansions."

"I know! Let's ride a paddleboat down the Mississippi River. We can look for alligators in the water," gabbed Joe.

9

Peter said, "I think we should go to a New England lighthouse."

"Why don't we put on hip boots and harvest cranberries in the bogs?" Joe asked. "Maybe we can take some home."

Peter said, "Why don't we go to New York City and visit all the museums?"

"If we go to New York,
I want to climb the Statue of
Liberty. I heard that her nose
is gigantic!" exclaimed Joe.

Peter said, "Why don't we go to see the San Francisco skyline?"

"Okay, okay. But could we at least hike across the Golden Gate Bridge? I promise I'll walk slow," whispered Joe.

Where do you think they will go?